YOU HAVE TO FUCKING LEAD

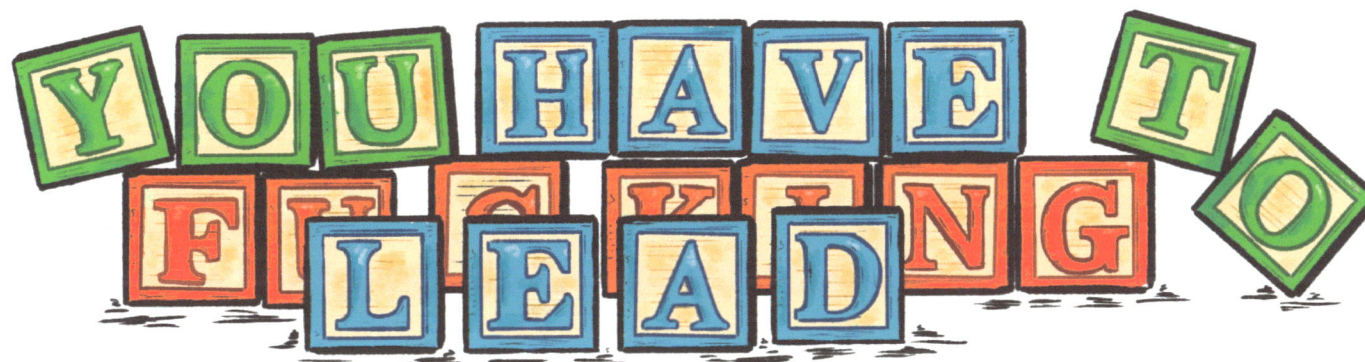

Written and illustrated by
John Spreincer McKellyanne Huckamucci

ISBN: 978-0-9885273-4-8

First edition October 2018.

Dedicated to everyone who ever "accidentally" stepped on a campaign yard sign while walking their dog.

Oh, are you mad about this dedication? ***SO DEEPLY SORRY.*** *Look, I don't support vandalism, but those things are hideous. You work yourself sick in order to secure a nice house with a beautiful lawn and then, instead of planting flowers or vegetables or even just putting a cute little bird feeder somewhere, you stab it with these impossibly ugly signs, all designed by graphic designers who equate "talent" with "number of different fonts I can cram into this small sign," and for what? Whose mind has ever been changed by a sign, especially an ugly sign? No one's, and you know that. You totally fucking know that. But you just stick that sign out there anyway because you want to piss off your neighbor two houses down who stuck the other party's sign on their once-inviting lawn to piss you off. You two deserve each other.*

Our president rages and tweets and gloats,
While our country, tired and angry, continues to regress.

The rich are eating the poor.
The middle class continues to bleed.
I know you're too arrogant to answer my question,
But remember that promise you made to lead?

I do. Like it was yesterday.
Because it fucking WAS yesterday.
In an editorial. In a speech.
On my TV. In my feed.

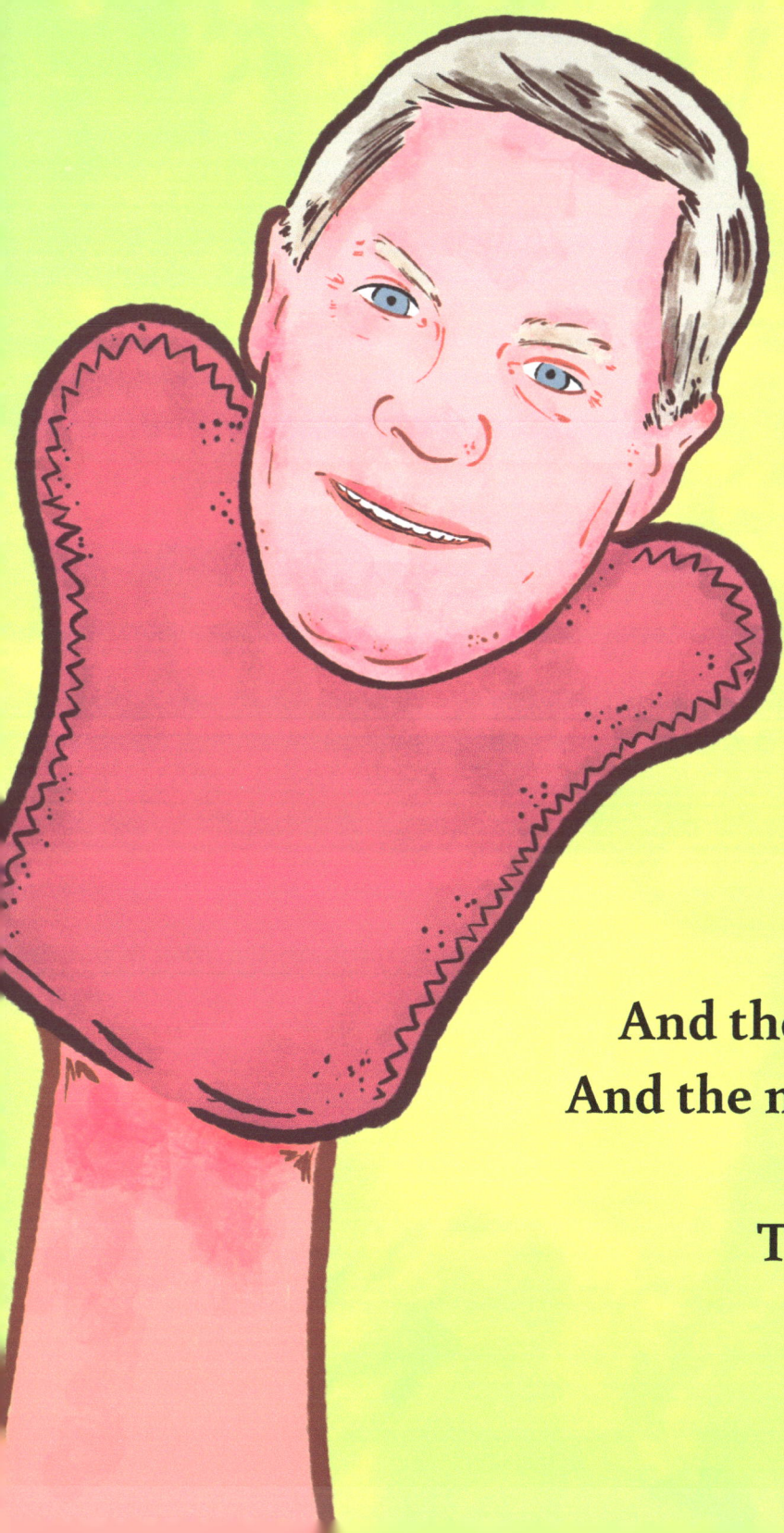

And the day before that, and the week before that,
And the month before that, and the year before that.
Is all this talking about doing your job
The reason you have no time to actually act?

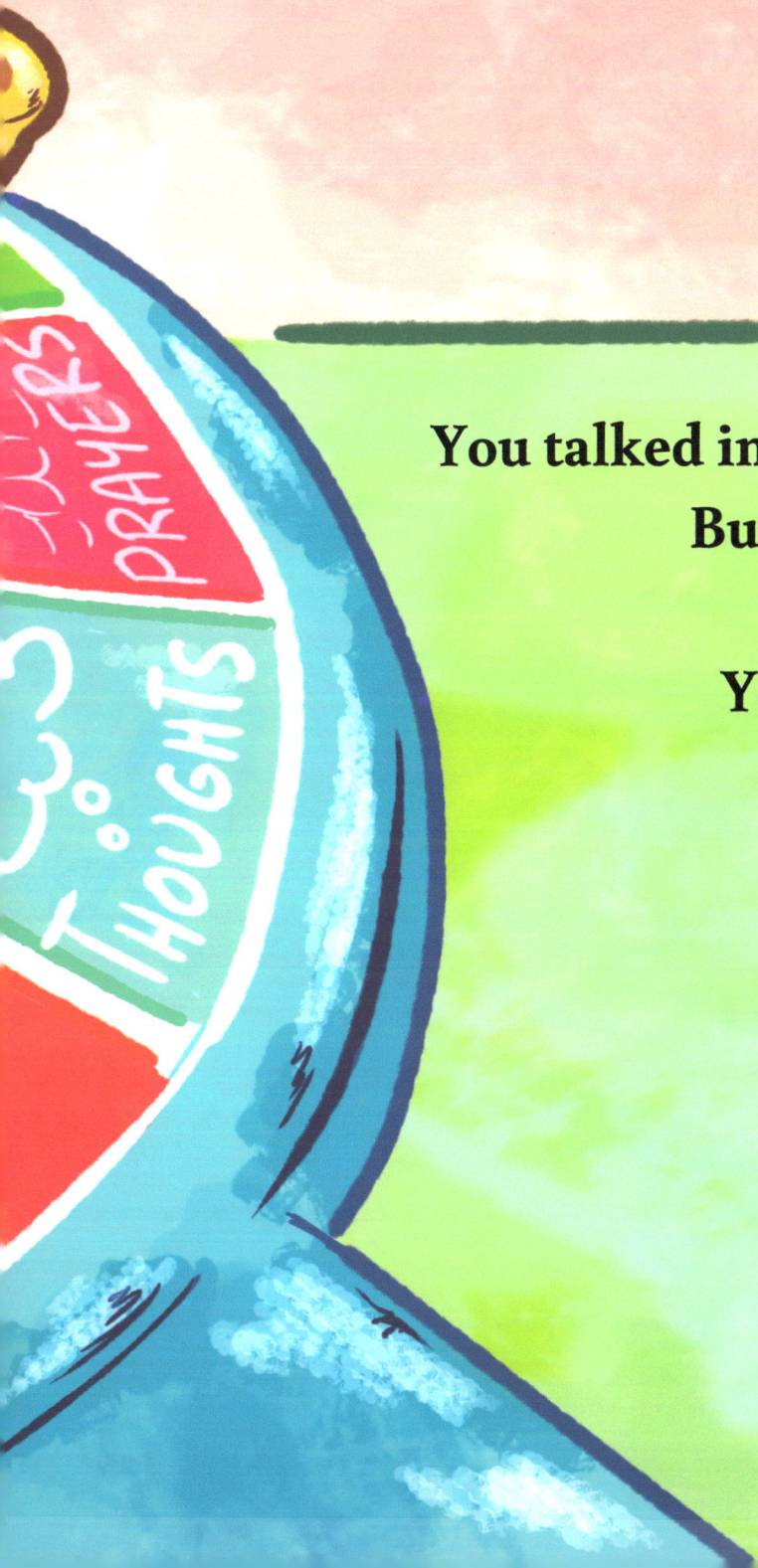

You talked incessantly about all these things we need to do.
But in case you've forgotten, we all voted for *you*.
And all these things you say we need to do,
You, yes *you*, have the power to actually pursue.
You know that everything I'm saying is true.
So what the fucking fuck is wrong with you?

What do you mean, "Things are great, by and large?"
Next to nothing has improved since you were elected to take charge.
When you ran, you wailed that the country needed fixing.

And everybody nodded and agreed.
Now that you can do the fixing,
You suddenly don't see the need?

Oh, the stock market's doing great?
Awesome. I have eight whole shares.
And that's eight more than most have,
Because you rail against wages that are fair.
You say the economy's never been better,
But everywhere I go I see folks in despair.
And for them, all you seem to ever spare
Are a bunch of no-cash-value thoughts and prayers.
Can I use Apple stock to pay for my care? I can't? No shit.
So when you brag about the markets, why the fuck should I even care?

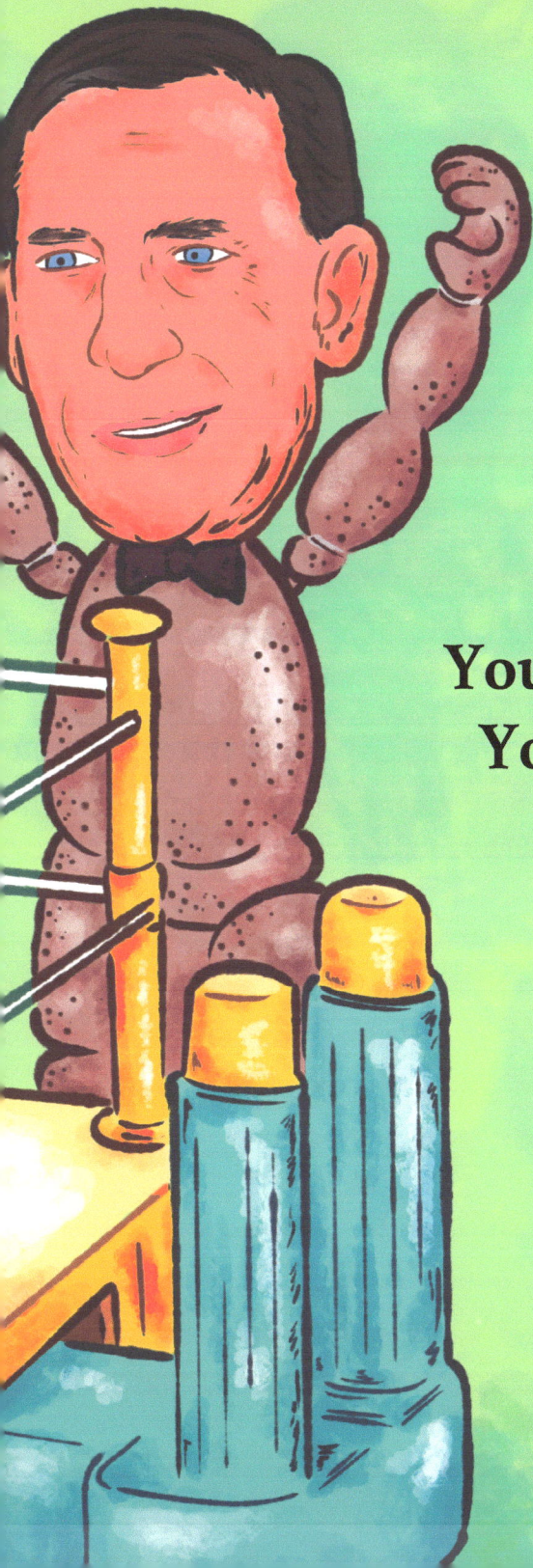

But this isn't about us. No, folks, it's about you.
Your words are relentless, but your actions are few.
You promised reform, and now refuse to perform,
And the bickering you once pledged to stop
Has instead become the norm.

Passing hastily-written bills while everyone's asleep,
Half-handwritten with scribbles everywhere, they're so crude.
You wouldn't let your kids hand in homework that looked this cheap,
So how in the world is it good enough for you?

Oh that's right, you're trying to please THIS idiot.
Seriously, he's a boob. We all know it. We know YOU know it. Cut the shit.
No sane person trusts him not to screw up everything that falls into his hands.
And when he does, he blames and calls you names and doesn't give a damn.

So WHY in the EVER LOVING FUCK
Can't you stand up to this clown?
What about him makes you so chicken-hearted and weak-kneed?
You're deathly afraid of a guy whose hair is literally glued to his crown,
And you want me to believe you can actually lead?

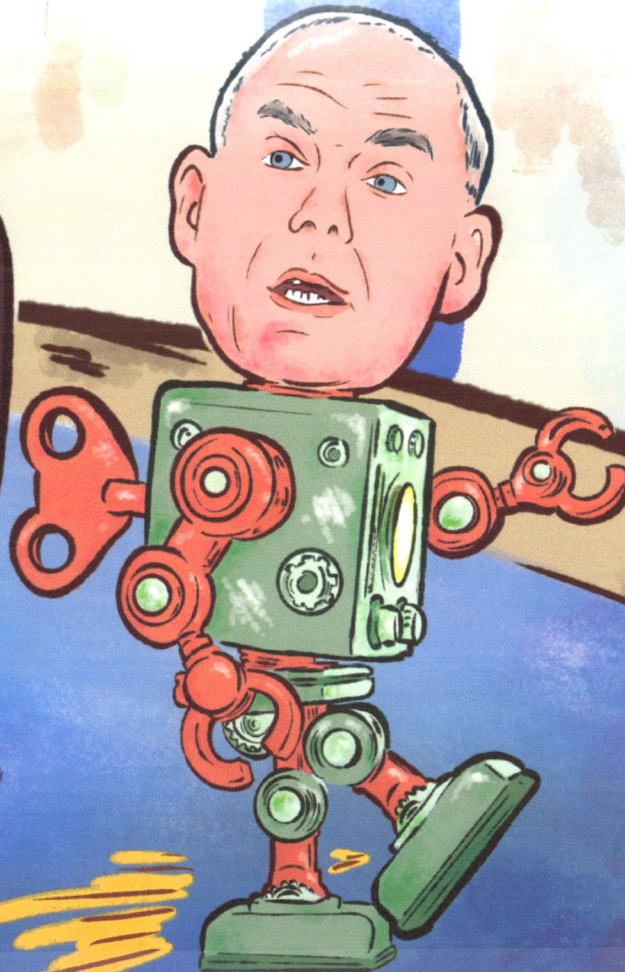

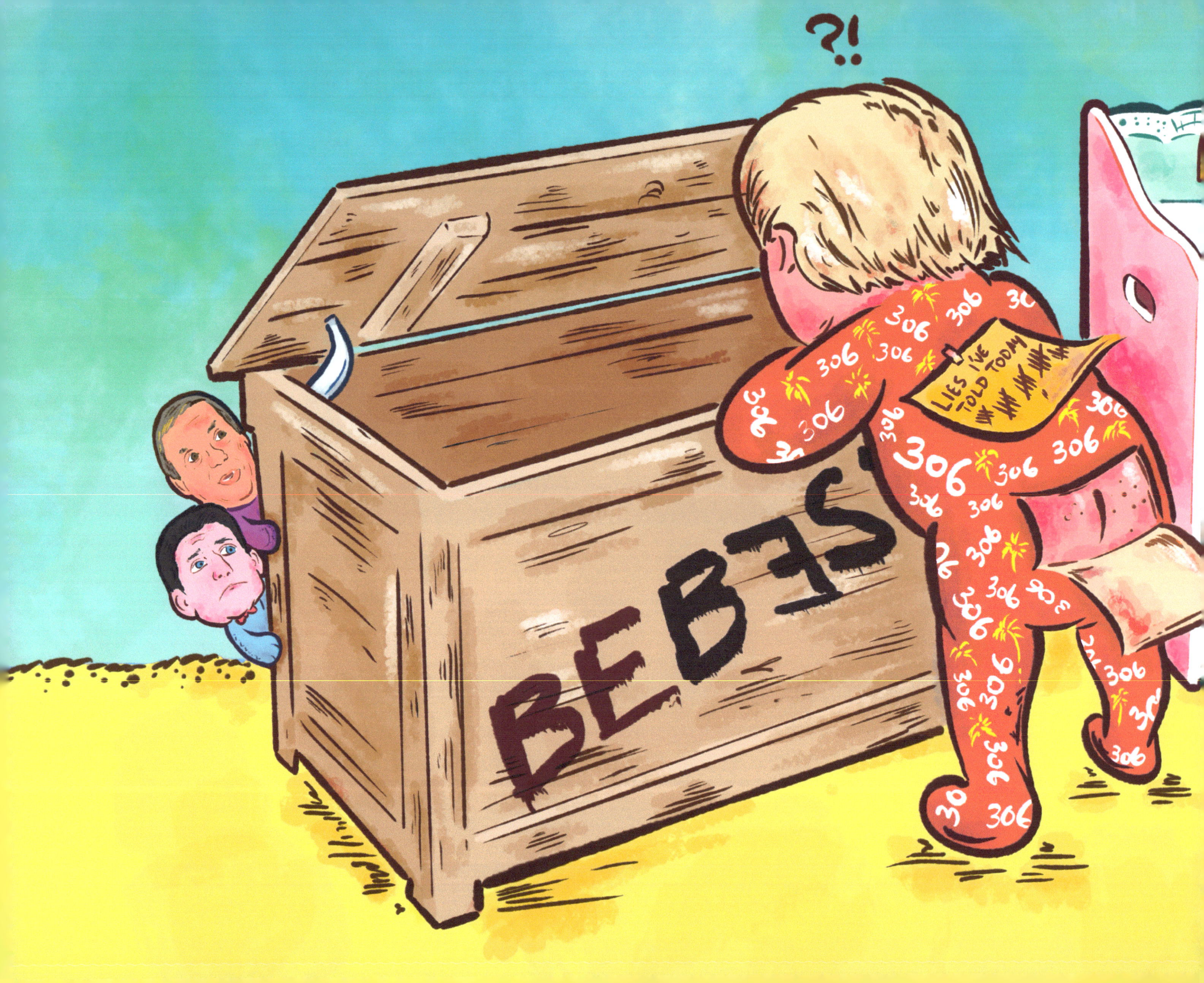
?!
BEBƎS
LIES I'VE TOLD TODAY
306

I guess you must be afraid, because you aren't even here.
Nor there. Nor anywhere. You've stopped pretending to care.
How many recesses a year does Congress get, anyway?
Even first graders do more work than you, and they play every day!

And wow, look at that, two whole years are just gone.
And now you're back to calling me at the crack of fucking dawn.
Making promises in my feeds and on the campaign trail.
More ads on TV, more flyers in the mail.

As a campaigner you're clutch, I'll give you that much,

In spite of how much you've fallen out of touch.

But do you actually expect to fool me twice, even one little bit,

When your actions this past year showed you don't give a shit?

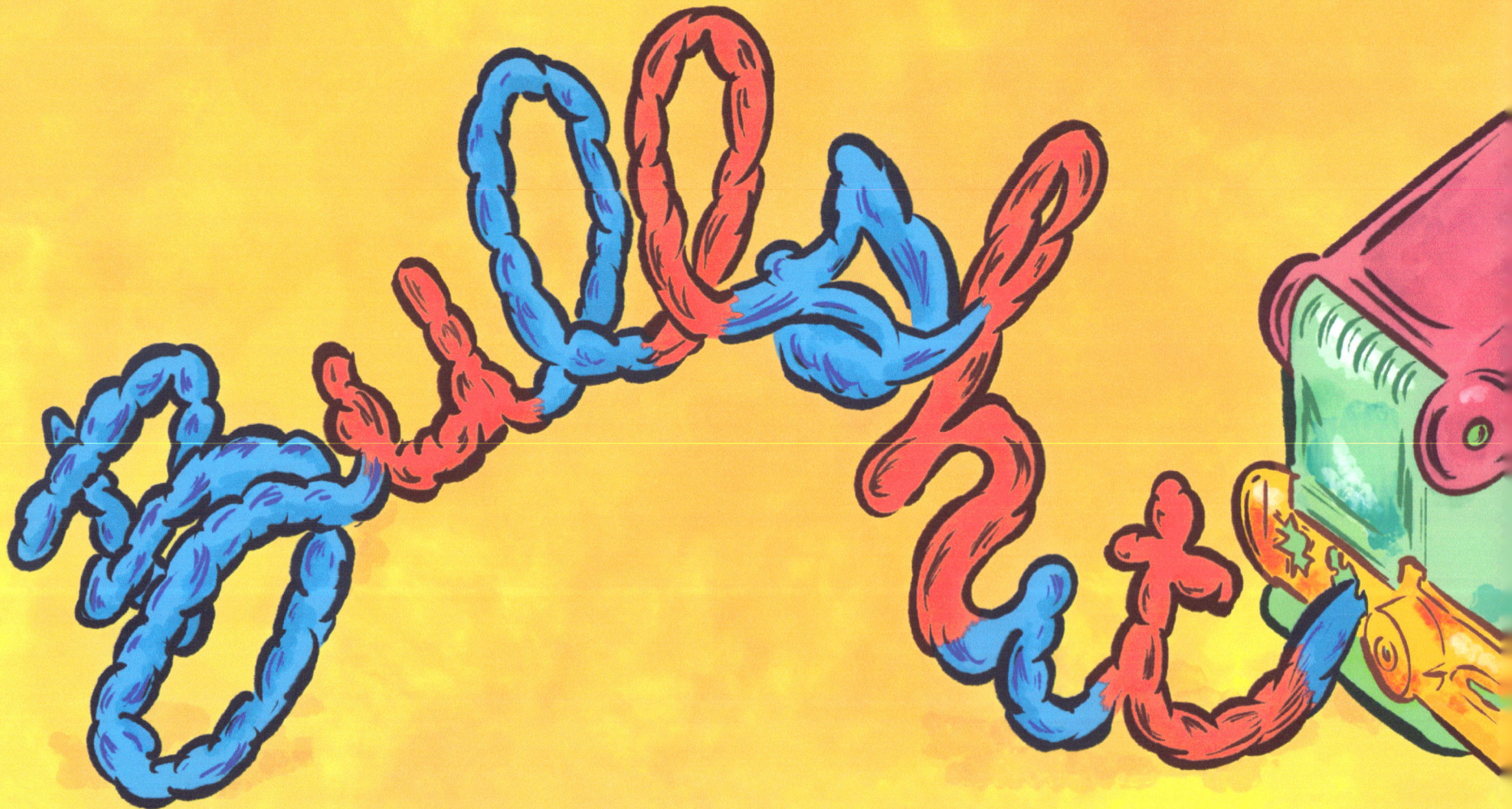

Stop. Enough.
You said that all before.
You've done enough damage already,
And you're asking us to let you do more?
Nope. Sorry, we're done here.
It's time for someone new.
And frankly, at this point,
I'd rather vote for anyone but you.

We need someone with backbone, common sense and grit,
To stand up to this clown and clean up all your shit.

That could've been you.
All you had to do was lead!

But you couldn't do even that.
So it's time to fucking leave.

About the Author

John Spreincer McKellyanne Huckamucci is ███████████████████████████████ ████████████████████████. ██████ hopes to have a career in cable news one day. ██████████ lives in Washington, D.C., and this is ██████ second ~~cry for help~~ book.

His first book, *Stop Fucking Tweeting and Go the Fuck to Sleep, Mr. President* (see shameless promotion, right), is in stores now, but filed under "humor" instead of "horror" or "non-fiction" for whatever reason.

www.ingramcontent.com/pod-product-compliance
Lightning Source LLC
Chambersburg PA
CBHW041552030426

42336CB00004B/55